The Missions of California

Mission
San Buenaventura

Amy Margaret

The Rosen Publishing Group's
PowerKids Press™
New York

To Gram and Gramps Hanson, with love

Published in 2000, 2003 by The Rosen Publishing Group, Inc.
29 East 21st Street, New York, NY 10010

Revised Edition 2003

Book Design: Danielle Primiceri

Photo Credits and Photo Illustrations: pp. 1, 4, 31, 51 © Shirley Jordan; pp. 5, 43 © SuperStock; p.6 © Robert Holmes/CORBIS; pp. 7, 10, 44, 45, 46 © CORBIS-Bettmann; p. 8, © Tim Hall; pp. 9A, 27 © Seaver Center for Western History Research, Los Angeles Museum of Natural History; p. 11 © courtesy of the Santa Barbara Trust for Historic Preservation; p. 12 © North Wind Picture Archive; pp. 13, 16, 19, 34, 35, 36, 37, 41 © Michael K. Ward; pp. 15, 17, 18, 21, 25, 30, 32, 38, 47, 48, 49 by Cristina Taccone; p. 20 © The Granger Collection, New York; pp. 39, 50 © The Bancroft Library; p. 40 Santa Barbara Historical Society; p. 42 © Department of Special Collections University of Southern California Libraries.

Editorial Consultant Coordinator: Karen Fontanetta, M.A., Curator, Mission San Miguel Arcángel
Editorial Consultant: Ann D. Snider
Historical Photo Consultants: Thomas L. Davis, M. Div., M.A.
                                   Michael K. Ward, M.A.

Margaret, Amy
   Mission San Buenaventura / by Amy Margaret
      p. cm.—(The missions of California)
   Includes index.
   ISBN 0-8239-5888-4 (lib. bdg.)
   1. San Buenaventura Mission—History. 2. Franciscans—California—Ventura Region—History. 3. Chumash Indians—Missions—California—Ventura Region—History. 4. Spanish mission buildings—California—Ventura Region—History. 5. California—History—To 1846.
   I. Title. II. Series: Missions of California (Rosen Publishing Group)
F869.S187M37 1998
979.4'92—dc21   98-46485
                                                           CIP

Contents

1 Spanish Explorers Arrive in California   5

2 The Chumash   14

3 Father of the California Missions: Junípero Serra   21

4 Founding and Building Mission San Buenaventura   26

5 Daily Life   33

6 Troubles at Mission San Buenaventura   38

7 The Secularization of the Missions   43

8 Mission San Buenaventura Today   48

9 Make Your Own Model Mission San   52
      Buenaventura

   Important Dates in Mission History   58

   Glossary   59

   Pronunciation Guide   61

   Resources   62

   Index   63

Spanish Explorers Arrive in California

Reminders of some of the richest moments in California's history can be found today in the 21 missions that lie along the state's west coast, from San Diego to Sonoma. Mission San Buenaventura has been a part of this landscape for more than 200 years.

The California missions were founded in the 1700s by Spanish friars, or *frays*, who hoped to spread their religion to the American Indians throughout America's west coast. The friars went to live in California to encourage the Indians to live with them and accept their Christian beliefs and European ways. They also hoped that the missions would expand the size and wealth of the Spanish empire. The story of the California missions lies not only in the work of the friars, but also in the struggles of the Indian populations who would, over time, be almost wiped out. The first mission was built in 1769, but events leading up to its founding started more than 200 years earlier, halfway around the world, in Spain.

The Age of Exploration

In 1493, Christopher Columbus brought back news of the New World (the areas we now know as South America, Central America, and North America) to Spain. Soon afterward, many European countries sent more explorers to learn about the New World and to claim areas of it for themselves. Many Europeans

▲
Christopher Columbus discovered the New World for the Europeans.

◄ *Mission San Buenaventura today, over 200 years after its founding.*

went to the New World hoping to find gold. Others hoped to find a river that could take them through the continent, connecting the Atlantic and Pacific Oceans. They thought that this would provide a faster way to get to Asia, where they could buy silks and spices to sell at home.

In the 1520s and 1530s, Spanish explorers and soldiers like Hernán Cortés and Francisco Pizarro conquered the great civilizations of the Aztecs and Incas in the lands that are now Mexico and Peru. This brought great wealth to Spain and allowed it to expand its empire. When Cortés conquered the area that is now Mexico, the Spanish named this area New Spain. By expanding from New Spain into other areas of North America, Spain hoped to grow even larger and wealthier.

Juan Rodríguez Cabrillo

Juan Rodríguez Cabrillo first visited the western coast of North America in 1542. This Spanish explorer was sent to find a river that joined the Pacific and Atlantic Oceans and to see if there were any great cities to conquer. He and his crew were also supposed to look for harbors where Spanish ships could rest on their long trips. Cabrillo and his crew sailed from New Spain, up the coast of Baja, or lower, California, and into Alta, or upper, California. Cabrillo claimed these coastal lands for Spain even though he found California Indians already living there.

In Alta California, shores were rocky, and it was difficult to find ports where ships could sail safely to shore. Cabrillo and his men found their first port in September 1542, in what is now San Diego Bay. Cabrillo and his crew continued sailing north, up the coast of Alta California. Cabrillo died in January 1543, partway through the voyage. After his death, Cabrillo's crew sailed as far north as the area that is now the state of Oregon. They proved that Alta California was not an island, as some had thought, but rather was part of a large mainland.

In April 1543, Cabrillo's crew returned to New Spain. They were sick and nearly starved. They had not found a river that ran through the continent nor any rich cities. In many ways their trip seemed like a failure, but it gave valuable information to the Spanish explorers who would eventually follow.

◀ *This is a statue of Spanish explorer Juan Rodríguez Cabrillo.*

The Europeans found many different tribes of people living in the New World. They called all these people "Indians" because this is what Christopher Columbus called them after his trip in 1492. At the time, Columbus thought he had sailed to Asia, which was then known as the Indies, so he mistakenly called the native people in the New World Indians.

Sebastián Vizcaíno

In 1602, 60 years after Cabrillo's expedition, Sebastián Vizcaíno was sent by ship from New Spain to look again for a connecting waterway between the Atlantic and Pacific Oceans. This trip was Vizcaíno's first attempt to land along Alta California's rocky shore. Only Cabrillo had successfully made it to land.

Vizcaíno's found a port during his journey. He named this port Monterey after the viceroy of New Spain. When Vizcaíno returned to New Spain, he told of all that he had found, particularly this new harbor and the California Indians, whom he described as being "friendly,

generous, and peaceful." However, the rulers of Spain still wanted to find a trade route connecting the Atlantic and Pacific Oceans. When both Cabrillo and Vizcaíno failed to find such a route, the rulers of Spain decided to stop funding these voyages. No Spanish ships sailed to California for the next 160 years.

Spain Takes Control of California

When both Russian and English rulers started sending ships to the western coast of North America, Spain became concerned that it would lose the land that Cabrillo and Vizcaíno had claimed more than 100 years earlier. Spain quickly took measures to permanently control the California land.

In 1769, New Spain's viceroy chose Captain Gaspár de Portolá to lead a group to establish religious settlements, or missions, in Alta California. Portolá sent three ships and two land expeditions from New Spain to the area that is today San

Captain Gaspár de Portolá

Diego. A friar named Fray Junípero Serra accompanied Portolá on one of the land groups, which left in March 1769. Along the way, the expedition parties met many Indians, particularly a group called the Chumash. The

Chumash were friendly, and they traded baskets and animal skins for European beads and ribbons. On July 16, 1769, Fray Serra founded Alta California's first mission, Mission San Diego de Alcalá. This was the first permanent European settlement in California.

Spain's Plan for California

Spanish rulers sent more explorers, friars, and soldiers to California with a plan to settle the area, which was already inhabited by various Native American tribes.

Each settlement would have three branches: religious, military, and civic. First the Spanish wanted to build missions, where California Indians could be converted to Christianity. The Spanish believed that only Christians would go to heaven after they died. They believed that the Indians would benefit greatly by giving up their own religious beliefs and adopting those of the Christians.

Fray Junípero Serra was known as the father of the missions.

The Spanish built four large presidios, or military forts, on the California coast. The presidios included housing for soldiers, warehouses, and storage spaces for gun powder. These forts were meant to protect the missions. Groups of soldiers from these

▲

Mission San Buenaventura was protected by the presidio of Santa Barbara. Santa Barbara's military district stretched from San Luis Obispo in the north to Los Angeles in the south. Today there are efforts to rebuild the presidio.

forts would stay at the missions. The soldiers would protect the friars from the possibility of Indian attacks and help enforce any rules that Spain would make for the settlers.

 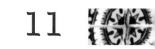

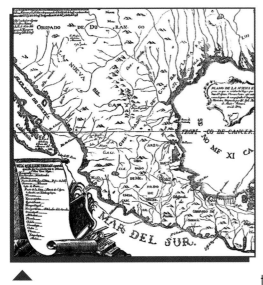

This is a map of New Spain.

Finally the Spanish would build agricultural towns called *pueblos*, where Spanish citizens from New Spain would be given land to live on and to farm. In addition to teaching the California Indians about Christianity, the missionaries planned to teach the Indians how to grow food, raise cattle and sheep, and make tools and crafts such as soap, candles, horseshoes, and leather goods. The missionaries believed that if the Indians learned how to grow their own food instead of having to hunt for it, they could live in permanent villages or towns and their children could attend school. The Spanish felt that their plans to train the Indians in their work methods and belief systems should take about 10 years. After these 10 years, the mission land and settlements would be turned over to the Indians to operate on their own as tax-paying Spanish citizens. This process was called secularization. Once the missionaries turned the land over to the Indians, the missionaries planned to travel to another area and train more Indians about the Spanish way of life. This may have seemed like a good plan, but it did not work out well.

The mission settlements marked the beginning of a period of change that would bring Europeans to California and end a way of life for the California Indians, who had lived there peacefully for many generations.

The Chumash Indians of California believed in spirits of good and evil. They also believed in many different gods.

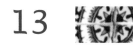

The Chumash

When Spanish explorers sailed to Alta California, California Indian tribes had been living there for thousands of years. At the time of exploration, Europeans believed that some races and groups of people were naturally better than others. The Spanish thought that they were smarter than the California Indians and that their Christian beliefs were the right beliefs. This feeling of superiority is one reason that the Spanish felt it was acceptable to take the Indians' land. The Spanish did not realize that the Indians had their own traditions and beliefs that were just as important as those of the Europeans. Today we value the differences between people that give our country and our world its diversity, but at that time, many Europeans believed that these differences only proved that the European cultures were better than others. Many Europeans felt that it was their responsibility to help others learn to adopt their lifestyle and religion. By trying to teach Indians the European ways of life, European settlers in the Americas helped to destroy the native cultures that had been in existence for thousands of years.

The Chumash Tradition

The Chumash were one of the California Indian groups that dwelled along the southern coast of Alta California. The Chumash did not farm. The men fished and hunted for small animals. The women gathered fruits, nuts, and vegetables. Nature provided the Chumash people with plenty of food so there was no need to plant or farm.

The Chumash Indians did not believe in the Christian god that Fray Serra and his companions said was the true god. The Indians' beliefs were quite different from the Europeans'. The Chumash believed in gods of

Chumash Indians played and danced together in their villages. ▶

the Sun and the Moon, who were their most powerful gods, and in other good and evil spirits.

Every Chumash village was led by a chief and a shaman. The chief was in charge of passing out food and valuables to the tribe members. He would also lead battles with other tribes or with the European settlers. The biggest disputes were usually over the control of land. The shaman was the religious leader of the village. The shaman gave advice and helped cure the sick. In some cases, the shaman performed rituals believed to bring rain. While men usually served in the chief and shaman positions, women sometimes held these roles as well.

The shaman was the religious leader of the Chumash village.

Every village had at least one *temescal*, or sweat lodge. This building was used by men before special religious ceremonies or hunting trips. They would sit naked in the small building in front of a blazing fire. *Temescals* were similar to today's saunas or steam rooms. After sweating and cleansing their bodies, the men would bathe in water to cool down. This process was also believed to cure illnesses.

The Chumash Home

The Chumash lived in dome-shaped houses made out of wood and reeds. These homes were often large, and some could hold as many as 50 people. To make a house, the Chumash shaped wood into thin poles. They bent the poles to create a rounded roof. Then Chumash workers covered the house with tule, which were reeds that were woven tightly to keep out wind and rain.

A Chumash home made from wood and grass. ▶

The Craftsmanship of the Chumash

Not only were the Chumash skilled at building homes, they were also known for building great boats, called *tomols*, that were quick and strong. They used the *tomols* to fish and travel. The *tomols* were built to hold up to 10 people.

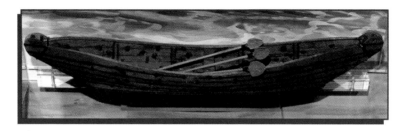

▲
The tomol *was a seaworthy boat which the Chumash used to fish and travel the Santa Barbara Channel and islands.*

▲
Chumash baskets are considered to be among the finest in the world.

18

The Chumash also wove fine baskets with beautiful patterns. These baskets were so well made that they were actually waterproof when the insides were coated with tar.

The Chumash traditions, beliefs, and skills were practically wiped out by the arrival of the Europeans. When the Spanish came to California, they brought diseases and new ways of life that would eventually destroy the Chumash.

Children in Chumash villages didn't go to school. Instead the older people in the village taught the boys and girls skills that they would need as they grew into adulthood. Boys were taught to hunt and make tools. Girls learned to weave baskets and find food.

American Indian children had time for fun, too. They played many games, such as tag, spinning tops, and a game that was similar to field hockey.

Father of the California Missions: Junípero Serra

In November 1713, Miguel José Serra was born to poor farmers in Majorca, an island off the coast of Spain. Even though his parents weren't educated, they wanted their son to learn to read and write. He went to school, where he was educated by Franciscan friars. They were called Franciscans because they followed the teachings of a man named Saint Francis of Assisi. While studying with these religious men, Miguel José decided that he wanted to be a priest. Miguel José also decided that he wanted to become a missionary and travel to foreign lands to convert people to Christianity.

This document was written by the U.S. Senate in 1963 to honor Fray Serra and his many accomplishments.

The Dream Begins

Miguel José joined the Franciscans and entered the convent of San Francisco. One of the customs of the Franciscans was to rename themselves after a Franciscan whom they admired. Serra chose the name of a man called Brother Junípero, who had been a close companion of Saint Francis of Assisi.

Fray Serra founded the first 9 of the 21 California missions.

21

Once he became a priest, Fray Junípero Serra taught classes. In 1749, he and two of his former students, Francisco Palóu and Juan Crespí, had the chance to follow their dreams of missionary work. Even though the missionary site in New Spain was thousands of miles (km) away and they would probably never return home again, they decided to go. Franciscans believed that to willingly accept a hard life showed a strong faith in God. They also felt that it was their duty to teach others about their religion.

The men sailed together across the Atlantic Ocean to New Spain. Once they arrived in the port city of Veracruz in New Spain, the missionaries still had close to 269 miles (433 km) to travel to reach their station in Mexico City.

New Spain

Fray Serra, Fray Palóu, and Fray Crespí walked for two weeks to reach the College of San Fernando in Mexico City. The friars walked on sand and dirt trails wearing wool robes and sandals. Despite their heavy clothing, the friars did not mind the heat or the walking. The Franciscans believed that they should be patient and accept the difficulties they would have to face in order to carry out their mission of spreading Christianity.

One evening as they were traveling, an insect bit Fray Serra on his left foot. The infection caused Serra a lot of pain, but eventually he convinced his companions that he was well enough to continue. The pain in his leg never left him, causing him to walk with a limp. Serra was proud of the suffering he had faced on the way to perform his religious work because he saw it as a necessary part of what God wanted him to do.

22

Baja California and Alta California

Once Serra arrived in Mexico City, he spent the next 17 years working for the College of San Fernando. In 1767, Fray Serra was sent by the college to Baja California (part of New Spain) to supervise 15 Spanish missions. A year later, Spain decided to strengthen its claim to Alta California, the land that today is the state of California. This event changed Fray Serra's life.

When Spain decided to build new missions in the uncharted Alta California, Serra was the best candidate for this large undertaking. He had done an excellent job supervising the Baja California missions and converting the Indians in that region. Finally, Serra would have his long-awaited

○ San Francisco Solano
○ San Rafael Arcángel
○ **San Francisco de Asís**
  ○ San José
    ○ **Santa Clara de Asís**
○ Santa Cruz
  ○ San Juan Bautista
   San Carlos Borromeo de Carmelo
○ Nuestra Señora de la Soledad

○ **San Antonio de Padua**
  ○ San Miguel Arcángel

○ **San Luis Obispo de Tolosa**

○ La Purísima Concepción
  ○ Santa Inés
    ○ Santa Bárbara
     ○ San Buenaventura

    ○ San Fernando Rey de España
     ○ **San Gabriel Arcángel**

○ San Juan Capistrano

○ San Luis Rey de Francia

○ **San Diego de Alcalá**

The California missions were built along the coast of California. The missions built before San Buenaventura are represented on this map in dark blue and the ones built after are in light gray.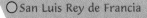

opportunity to travel to places never visited by other missionaries.

Fray Serra was made mission president. His job was to establish the missions in Alta California, make sure that each mission had everything that it needed, and oversee the friars who would run each mission. He worked hard for 15 years, founding nine missions and baptizing more than 6,000 California Indians. Baptism is the ceremony that is performed when someone is accepted into the Christian faith. Two years after founding Mission San Buenaventura, Fray Serra died. Fray Francisco Palóu wrote that mission bells sounded at Serra's passing. Sailors, soldiers, settlers, priests, friars, and over 600 Indians attended his funeral. Many people mourned the loss of their beloved friar. Today Fray Junípero Serra is a candidate for Catholic sainthood, an honor given by the Catholic Church to someone who has shown an incredible devotion to God. The Spanish government's first plans were to build a mission in the south (San Diego) and then in the north (Monterey) of Alta California. Another was to be built around the Ventura area. After the first three were established, others would be built in between them along the coast. The road that would eventually connect all 21 missions along the coast of Alta California was called El Camino Real, or the Royal Road.

When missionaries were looking for places to build their missions, they had very specific needs. To get approval from the viceroys of New Spain, an area had to have lots of fresh water for drinking and watering the crops, rich soil that could be used for livestock grazing and farming, and wood for constructing buildings and making tools and furniture.

The viceroys also said that the area had to have a large number of California Indians living there. One reason for this was that the missionaries needed to be near the people that they wanted to convert to Christianity. Another reason was that they could not have built their missions or farmed the land without the help of the Indians. Most missions had only two priests and five or six soldiers. This was not enough people to do the work involved in building or maintaining a mission. The missionaries needed Indians to work for them if they were to survive and be successful.

▲
Surrounded by three of his fellow friars, Fray Serra is shown in death with a sleeping California brown bear cub at his feet. The bear cub represents a young California which would grow in time to become the most populated state in the Union.

Founding and Building
Mission San Buenaventura

The Beginning of San Buenaventura

Along with about 80 soldiers and their families, Fray Serra arrived at the site of the future San Buenaventura mission, near a Chumash village. Fray Serra founded this ninth mission on March 31, 1782. It would be the last mission he would found before his death in 1784. On that memorable Easter morning, the group held a ceremony and raised a large wooden cross to mark the site of the mission.

Attracting Converts

Once the missionaries had completed their founding ceremony, they were left with a cross in the ground and no mission. To get their religious work started and their mission built, the missionaries needed to attract the nearby Chumash and try to convert them. Often members of nearby tribes came to watch the founding ceremony and the preparations for the building of a mission. The missionaries gave food, beads, and trinkets to the Indians who helped them with their work, and this often encouraged more Indians to come and work for the Spanish. As they continued to work together and the Indians were continually rewarded with gifts, the missionaries encouraged the Indians to build new houses that were closer to the mission site. Eventually the friars would start to teach them about the Christian religion.

Converting the California Indians

Once the California Indians had come to rely on the Spanish for food and gifts, the friars began to teach them about Christianity. This was often difficult since neither the friars nor the Indians knew one

It took a lot of hard work for the Chumash Indians and the Spanish to build Mission San Buenaventura. ▶

another's language. Slowly, though, they learned to communicate. When the friars felt that the Indians were ready to be baptized, they held a ceremony in which the Indians were blessed with water. The ceremony of baptism meant that they were now Christians and would no longer practice their own religion. The friars called the newly converted Christians, neophytes. Before the Indians were baptized, they were told that once they became neophytes, they would no longer be allowed to leave the mission without permission. If they tried to escape, they would be brought back and punished by the soldiers.

While we know a lot about why the missionaries wanted to convert the California Indians, we do not know much about why many Indians agreed to be converted. This is because the Indians did not keep written records for us to read today. It may be that the Indians who agreed to be baptized did it because they were convinced that Christianity was the right religion, or it may be that they liked the gifts of the Spanish and wanted to keep receiving them. In some cases, Indians may have converted because they were afraid that if they chose not to, they would be punished.

Building San Buenaventura

The buildings at San Buenaventura were built over a 50-year period, but most of them were constructed between 1790 and 1810. The first buildings at San Buenaventura were temporary shelters made of wood and reeds. They were used until permanent adobe structures, which took a lot more time to build, were finished.

To make adobe buildings, the neophytes had to first make adobe bricks. Adobe is made of a mixture of clay, water, and straw. The neophytes dug a hole in the ground and placed the clay in it. When water was added, the clay became sticky. Finally straw was mixed in to make the bricks stronger. To stir the large batch of adobe, the neophytes stepped into the hole and mixed it with their feet.

Once the adobe was mixed, it was poured into wooden molds, where it hardened into bricks. The bricks were left to dry in the sun until they were ready for use. To build walls, the neophytes stacked the bricks on top of one another and cemented each layer with mud. The walls that were built with these bricks were six feet (1.8 m) thick.

At first mud and straw were used to make the mission roofs. Straw burned quickly though, and these roofs were easily damaged by heavy rains. This is why the straw roofs were later replaced with tiles.

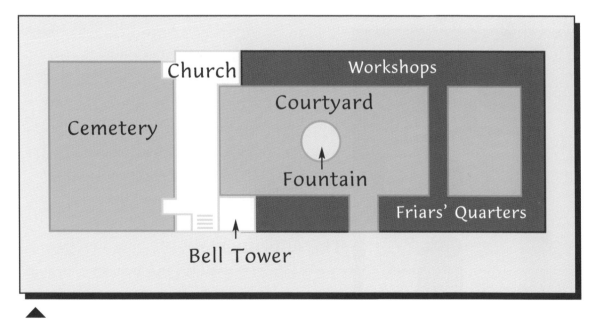

▲
This is the layout of Mission San Buenaventura.

29

San Buenaventura was designed like many of the other California missions. The buildings were set up around an open square, or quadrangle. The church served as one wall of the quadrangle and was always one of the first buildings to be built.

Other buildings around the square included living quarters for the friars and visitors, rooms called *monjeríos* for unmarried women and girls over the age of 11, rooms for unmarried men, storage rooms, the kitchen and dining rooms, and workrooms.

Next to the quadrangle was a small village, or *ranchería*, where married Indians and their small children lived. Soldiers also had housing next to the mission. From their quarters, the soldiers could view the church, the friars' rooms, and the *ranchería*. If the neophytes tried to escape from the mission or attack the friars, the soldiers would be able to see them.

San Buenaventura had a beautiful bell tower. It was the only mission to house wooden bells in addition to the more common metal bells. No one knows for sure why Mission San Buenaventura had wooden bells. Some people think that the wooden bells were used for Holy week when the metal bells were kept quiet.

The Aqueduct

All the missions had to develop a system for carrying water throughout the mission grounds. The Chumash at San Buenaventura

▲
The unique bell tower at Mission San Buenaventura.

constructed a sophisticated irrigation system that was seven miles (11.3 km) long.

A friar named Fray Pedro Benito Cambon designed the water system, or aqueduct. It was built using logs and stones to direct water from the Ventura River to the mission. About 10 years after the mission's founding, engineers from New Spain arrived to show the friars and neophytes how to make the system stronger. Today the design and construction of this aqueduct from natural materials is recognized as an engineering feat.

The finished aqueduct featured a filtration system for purifying drinking water. It also had reservoirs and valves that controlled the amount of water that flowed into the fields

▲
San Buenaventura was the only California mission to have wooden bells.

and five separate fountains for drinking and washing. The mission population could easily get drinking water, wash their clothes, and water their crops without leaving the mission grounds.

▲
The mission fountain was part of an extensive water system at mission San Buenaventura.

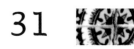

Daily Life

Routines

While the friars relied on the Chumash to do much of the mission's construction, the Chumash also had other chores. Every day started and ended with ringing church bells. A typical day would go like this:

Sunrise	Everyone woke up and went to the mission church to pray.
1 hour later	A bell rang for breakfast.
7 A.M.	A bell rang to send neophytes to work.
12 noon to 2 P.M.	Neophytes ate their meal and had a rest, or *siesta*.
2 P.M.	Everyone went back to work.
5 P.M.	The friars held prayers and devotions.
6 P.M.	Supper, then free time.
8 P.M.	Bedtime for women.
9 P.M.	Bedtime for men.

Like their days before the mission, Chumash women were primarily responsible for preparing food. To prepare food, they had to adapt to different ingredients and cooking methods introduced by the Spanish. The Chumash women were also taught how to weave and to make candles, soap, and clothing. Unmarried Chumash girls and women were locked in the *monjeríos* at night.

The men learned leatherwork, wood crafting, and farming. They planted grapes, which were native to the area. The Chumash also raised barley, oats, wheat, and oranges, which were all introduced by the

◄ *The Chumash learned how to make adobe bricks and roof tiles from the friars.*

The friars taught religious lessons to the Indians.

Spanish. One of the most profitable industries at Mission San Buenaventura was cattle raising. The meat from cattle was used for food, hides were used to make leather, and the fat was used to make candles and soap.

Children also had jobs at the mission. Some helped the women weave baskets or clothing. Others kept birds and animals away from the crops and the wet adobe bricks.

The friars also worked. In the morning and again in the afternoon, one friar taught lessons about the Catholic religion to all children over the age of five. After giving morning lessons, the friars toured the mission. They made sure everyone was doing his or her work and that no one had escaped.

Forced to live and work at the mission after being baptized, and unable to return to their homes except for short visits a few times each year, some neophytes became angry at their lack of freedom. Many tried to run away. Some succeeded in escaping, while others were brought back and beaten by Spanish soldiers. The more the neophytes were punished, the angrier they became.

▲

After a period of instruction, which lasted two years, the friars would baptize those Indians who wanted to become Christian.

Some of the Spanish soldiers treated the Indians terribly, abusing Indian women and beating some men to death. The friars tried to stop this harsh behavior. In the 1770s, Fray Serra tried hard. He traveled to New Spain to talk to government officials about this problem. Fray Serra took a young Indian boy named Juan Evangelista with him. They returned from New Spain with a document stating that missionaries could take control of the Indians away from the soldiers. This document is now considered to be an American Indian Bill of Rights. Many soldiers ignored the order and continued the cruel treatment.

One of the most influential people at Mission San Buenaventura was Fray José Señán. In 1806, he took charge of San Buenaventura, where he remained until his death in 1823. He allowed the Chumash to hold on to parts of their culture that other friars had banned. He realized that if he wanted to keep the neophytes at the mission, he would have to allow them to practice some of their traditions. Fray Señán allowed them to visit their villages and gave them permission to build *temescals* near the mission for their rituals.

Neophytes regularly visited their villages. The friars believed that they could influence others to consider joining their mission. ▶

Chumash rituals, like this dance, had once been banned at the mission.

Troubles at Mission San Buenaventura

Like the other missions, San Buenaventura had its share of both manmade and natural problems. The mission buildings had been complete for only three years when an earthquake damaged them in 1812. The aqueduct was also partially destroyed. While the church was being repaired, the neophytes built a temporary church a few miles (km) from the coast. This church was used for a year while the permanent structures were under repair.

Six years later, this temporary building was used again by the friars and neophytes to hide from a French pirate named Hippolyte de Bouchard. Bouchard had already done much damage to Mission San Juan Capistrano and the Monterey presidio. The friars heard a rumor that Bouchard was headed straight for Mission San Buenaventura. The friars ordered the neophytes to bury or hide the mission's valuables in caves. Then everyone living at the mission hid inland for a month. When they returned to the mission, they learned that Bouchard had sailed right past the Ventura area and nothing had been taken or destroyed.

This is a piece of Mission San Buenaventura's wall painted by Chumash Indians.

While the friars at San Buenaventura feared earthquakes and even pirates, the real trouble was at the mission itself. Some of the Chumash Indians had adapted well to their new life. They liked not having to worry about finding food, and living at the

Mission San Buenaventura became ▶ *damaged over the years.*

38

▲
The Indian villages were next to the mission. They did not have to travel a long distance to their home village.

mission protected them from their enemies. They felt that the friars were kind to them. Many developed good relationships with the friars. Others, however, were angry about losing their freedom. They didn't like being told by the friars when to wake up, eat, pray, work, and go to bed. Before living at the mission, the Chumash were used to moving around to different locations in search of food. They were also used to a way of life that was controlled by the things they needed, not by a schedule.

One of the biggest problems faced by the California Indians was disease. When the Spanish came over from Europe, they brought illnesses such as measles, smallpox, syphilis, pneumonia, and mumps. The

40

Indians had never been exposed to these diseases, so hundreds of thousands died. Due to these diseases, it is estimated that the California Indian population declined from 300,000 to approximately 30,000 by the 1850s.

Membership at the San Buenaventura mission reached its peak in 1816. At this time there were 1,328 neophytes at the mission. The measles epidemic of the 1820s caused the Chumash population to decrease dramatically. When the mission closed in 1834, only 636 neophytes were left.

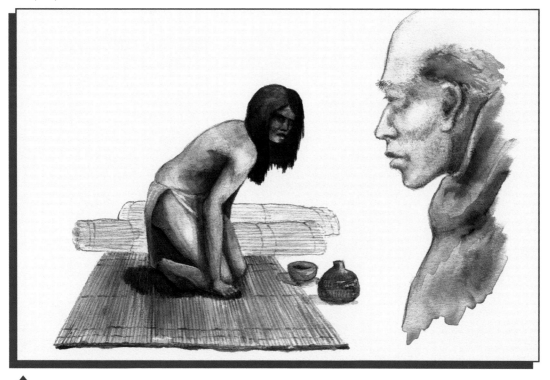

▲

Many Chumash became sick and died from diseases unknowingly brought to the New World by Europeans.

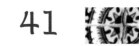

The Secularization of the Missions

In 1821, after 11 years of civil war, New Spain became a separate country from Spain and was renamed Mexico. The 21 Alta California missions now fell under the authority of the Mexican government. The Mexicans wanted to send more of their people into Alta California to claim and settle the land. They planned to secularize the missions and use the rich land for themselves. This would mean taking the missions away from the Catholic friars and replacing them with priests who did not do missionary work. The mission lands would be controlled by the government. The neophytes would no longer have to obey the friars, but they would have to obey Mexican officials.

The missionaries, who would lose all they had worked for over the years, were against secularization. They thought the neophytes would be unable to survive on their own after living for so long at the missions. While some neophytes did end up working in and around Mission San Buenaventura, some of the Chumash who had converted to Catholicism decided to return to their old villages and ways of life. However, it was not easy to make their old ways of life work again. Many Chumash were sick from European diseases. Many children had grown up with Christian, not Chumash, traditions. Homes, families, and friendships had to be rebuilt. More importantly, settlers now lived on their land. The Chumash were never able to fully regain their old ways of life. Too much had changed and too much had been lost.

In 1834, the Mexican government decided that the secularized missions were not successful enough to maintain. The missions could not provide the food and clothing needed for nearby settlers. Times were changing, too. American settlers from the east coast began moving into the

◀ *The Chumash and the Spanish worked together to build a mission.*

This shows pioneers on their way to California to search for gold.

area. Mexico began to lose its hold over Alta California. In 1843, the Mexican government gave some of the missions, including San Buenaventura, back to the Franciscan friars. Mexican officials believed the friars could make the missions successful again.

The Franciscans, however, were not given the chance to help at San Buenaventura. In 1846, a Mexican governor sold San Buenaventura to a man named José Arnaz. Mexico continued to lose control over Alta California. The United States and Mexico soon fought a war over the territory. This war is known as the Mexican War. The Americans won the war in 1848. Later that same year, settlers discovered gold in California. This brought thousands of new settlers to the territory in search of riches. Finally in 1850, under the leadership of President Millard Fillmore, California became the 31st state of the United States.

▲

President Millard Fillmore was the 13th president of the United States.

President Abraham Lincoln was the 16th president of the United States.

Several years later, in 1862, President Abraham Lincoln gave the California missions back to the Catholic Church. By this time, many of the missions were falling apart. San Buenaventura, however, continued to hold church services. Throughout all the changes in ownership, San Buenaventura kept its church doors open. They closed only once, for four months of restoration. They are still open today.

▲
Many people visit Mission San Buenaventura.

 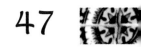

Mission San Buenaventura Today

Today Mission San Buenaventura sits on Ventura's Main Street, a busy thoroughfare for beach traffic. Mass is held at the mission seven mornings a week. Right next door to the mission is Holy Cross School, built in 1922.

Once a week, children enter the original sanctuary for Mass, where they sing and pray surrounded by California's rich history. In front of the school is a life-sized statue of Fray Junípero Serra. You can compare your height to his five-foot, two-inch (1.58 m) frame.

On the other side of the mission is its museum and gift shop. The museum contains artifacts such as vestments worn by the missionaries, the two original wooden bells, baskets woven by Chumash women, and many other objects that were a part of life at San Buenaventura.

The gardens of the mission are well kept, and you'll find a running fountain, an old olive press, and a water pump.

Near the mission are two other museums that contain artifacts that are related to Mission San Buenaventura. The Albinger

▲
Chumash basket, settling tank, and tools used by the Chumash Indians

Mission San Buenaventura on ▶ *Main Street today*

48

▲

The old mission church at San Buenaventura is now a parish church.

Archaeological Museum features pottery and other artifacts dug up in the area, as well as the original foundations of some of the buildings. Right across the street is the Ventura Museum of Natural History, which houses artifacts made by the Chumash Indians.

 50

Mission San Buenaventura is an important part of California's history.

Make Your Own Model
Mission San Buenaventura

To make your own model of Mission San Buenaventura, you will need:

cardboard	toothpicks	lasagne
ruler	paint (white, red)	glue
scissors	sand	moss
tape		

Directions

Step 1: Cut a piece of cardboard to measure 18" x 24" (45.7 x 60.9 cm) for your base.

18" (45.7 cm)

24" (60.9 cm)

Adult supervision is suggested.

Step 2: Cut two pieces of cardboard 4″ x 20″ (10.2 x 50.8 cm). Cut another two pieces of cardboard to measure 4″ x 15″ (10.2 x 38.1 cm). Tape together into a rectangular shape.

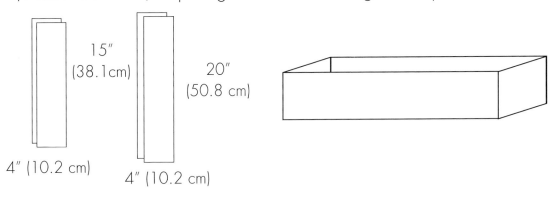

15″
(38.1cm)

20″
(50.8 cm)

4″ (10.2 cm)

4″ (10.2 cm)

Step 3: Use tape to secure the walls to the base.

Step 4: Now cut two pieces of cardboard to measure 4″ x 9″ (10.2 x 22.8 cm). Cut another two pieces of cardboard to measure 4″ x 14″ (10.2 x 35.6 cm). Tape these pieces together to form a rectangle. Place this rectangle inside the bigger rectangle and secure with tape.

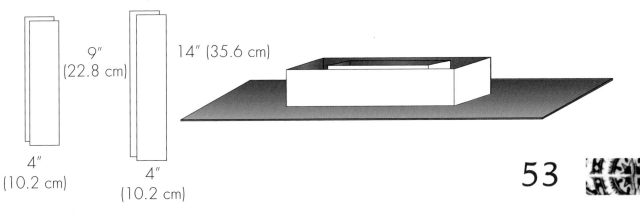

9″
(22.8 cm)

14″ (35.6 cm)

4″
(10.2 cm)

4″
(10.2 cm)

Step 5: To build the church, cut out a square piece of cardboard to measure 8.5" x 8.5" (21.6 x 21.6 cm). Cut this square diagonally to make two equal triangles of the same size.

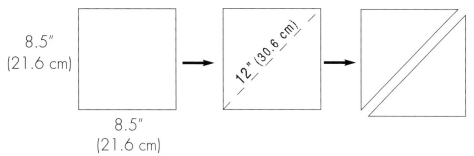

8.5"
(21.6 cm)

8.5"
(21.6 cm)

12" (30.6 cm)

Step 6: Attach one triangle with tape to the far right side of the mission from the inside wall to the outside wall as shown. Use tape to attach it. Tape a toothpick to the inside wall to prevent the triangle from falling.

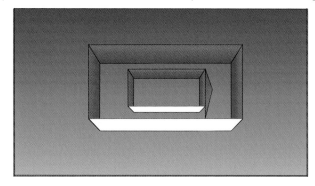

Step 7: Do the same thing with the other triangle, attaching it to the outside wall.

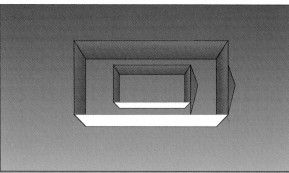

Step 8: To make a bell tower, cut three pieces of cardboard to measure 3″ x 12″ (7.6 x 30.6 cm). Fold each piece of cardboard every 3″ (7.6 cm) into the shape of a box.

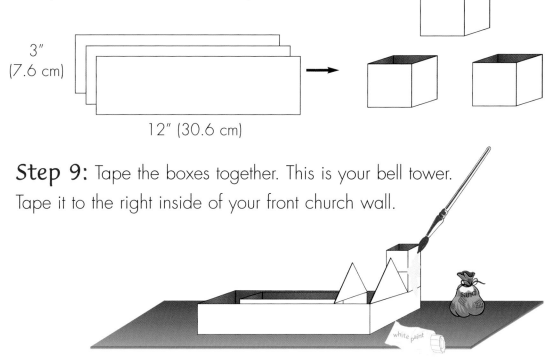

3″
(7.6 cm)

12″ (30.6 cm)

Step 9: Tape the boxes together. This is your bell tower. Tape it to the right inside of your front church wall.

Step 10: Paint the entire mission with white paint mixed with a little sand to give it texture. Let dry.

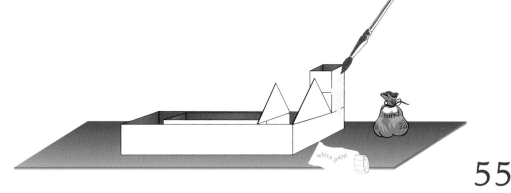

55

Step 11: Paint the dry lasagne with red paint. Let dry.

Step 12: Glue the dry lasagne to the tops of your walls.

Step 13: Paint a bell on the bell tower and paint windows and doors on the front of the church. Glue two toothpicks together to make a cross.

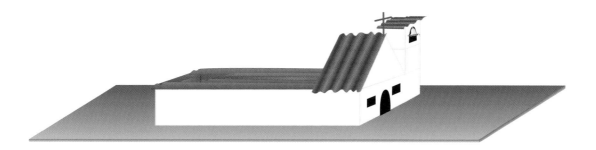

Step 14: Glue moss around the mission to look like grass. Add small branches for trees and small dried flowers.

*Use the above mission as a reference for building your mission.

Important Dates in Mission History

1492	Christopher Columbus reaches the West Indies
1542	Cabrillo's expedition to California
1602	Sebastián Vizcaíno sails to California
1713	Fray Junípero Serra is born
1769	Founding of San Diego de Alcalá
1770	Founding of San Carlos Borromeo de Carmelo
1771	Founding of San Antonio de Padua and San Gabriel Arcángel
1772	Founding of San Luis Obispo de Tolosa
1775–76	Founding of San Juan Capistrano
1776	Founding of San Francisco de Asís
1776	Declaration of Independence is signed
1777	Founding of Santa Clara de Asís
1782	**Founding of San Buenaventura**
1784	Fray Serra dies
1786	Founding of Santa Bárbara
1787	Founding of La Purísima Concepción
1791	Founding of Santa Cruz and Nuestra Señora de la Soledad
1797	Founding of San José, San Juan Bautista, San Miguel Arcángel, and San Fernando Rey de España
1798	Founding of San Luis Rey de Francia
1804	Founding of Santa Inés
1817	Founding of San Rafael Arcángel
1823	Founding of San Francisco Solano
1848	Gold found in northern California
1850	California becomes the 31st state

Glossary

adobe (uh-DOH-bee) Sun-dried brick made of straw, mud, and sometimes manure.

Alta California (AL-tuh ka-lih-FOR-nyuh) The area where the Spanish settled and built missions, today known as the state of California.

Baja California (BAH-ha ka-lih-FOR-nyuh) The Mexican peninsula directly south of the state of California.

baptism (BAP-tih-zum) A ceremony performed to accept someone into the Christian faith, intended to cleanse the convert of his or her sins.

Christian (KRIS-chun) Someone who follows the Christian religion or the teachings of Jesus Christ and the Bible.

convert (kun-VURT) To change religious beliefs.

crucifix (KROO-suh-fiks) A statue of Jesus Christ on the cross.

Franciscan (fran-SIS-kin) A member of a Catholic religious group started by Saint Francis of Assisi in 1209.

missionary (MIH-shuh-nayr-ee) A person who teaches his or her religion to people with different beliefs.

neophyte (NEE-oh-fyt) A California Indian who has converted to another religion.

New Spain (NOO SPAYN) The area where the Spanish colonists had their capital in North America and that would later become Mexico.

quadrangle (KWAH-drang-ul) The square at the center of a mission that is surrounded by four buildings.

secularization (seh-kyoo-luh-rih-ZAY-shun) When the operation of the mission lands was taken away from the church and given to the government.

viceroy (VYS-roy) The governor of a place who rules there as a representative of the king.

Pronunciation Guide

Chumash (CHOO-mash)

monjerío (mohn-hayr-EE-oh)

pueblo (PWAY-bloh)

ranchería (ran-chuh-REE-ah)

siesta (see-EHS-tah)

temescal (TEH-mes-cal)

tomol (TOH-mul)

Resources

To learn more about the California missions, check out these books, Web sites, and museums:

Books

Genet, Donna. *Father Junípero Serra: Founder of the California Missions.* Springfield, NJ: Enslow Publishers, 1996.

Hogan, Elizabeth, editor. *The California Missions.* Menlo Park, CA: Sunset Publishing, 1991.

Web Sites

Due to the changing nature of Internet links, PowerKids Press has developed an online list of Web sites related to the subject of this book. This site is updated regularly. Please use this link to access the list:
www.powerkidslinks.com/moca/msbuenav/

Museums

If you live anywhere near the Ventura area or are planning to visit, you may have the opportunity to do some up close research. Here are the primary places that you might want to visit, along with phone numbers so that you can verify hours or ask questions.

Mission San Buenaventura	Chumash Interpretative Center	The Ventura Museum of History	Albinger Archaeological Museum
211 E. Main Street	3290 Lang Ranch Parkway	100 E. Main Street	113 E. Main Street
Ventura, CA 93001	Thousand Oaks,	Ventura, CA 93001	Ventura, CA 93001
(805) 643-4318	CA 91362	(805) 653-0323	(805) 648-5823
	(805) 492-8076		

Index

A

adobe, 28–29, 34
Alta California, 6–8, 9, 10, 12, 14, 23–24, 43–45
Arnaz, José, 45
aqueduct, 30–31, 38

B

Baja California, 6, 23
baptism, 24, 28, 35
Bouchard, Hippolyte de, 38

C

Cabrillo, Juan Rodríguez, 6–9
Cambon, Fray Pedro Benito, 31
Christianity, 5, 10–12, 14, 21, 22, 24
    converting Indians to, 12, 14, 15, 21–22, 23, 25–26, 28, 43
Chumash Indians, 10, 14, 16–19, 26, 28, 30, 38, 40–41, 43–44
    craftsmanship, 18–19, 33, 48
    culture, 14, 16–19, 36, 48–50
    homes, 17–18
    life in the mission, 33–36
Columbus, Christopher, 5
Cortés, Hernán, 6
Crespí, Juan, 22

D

diseases, 19, 40–41, 43

E

Evangelista, Juan, 36
explorers, 5–9, 10, 14

F

Fillmore, Millard, 45
Franciscan friars, 5, 10, 21–22, 24, 26, 28, 30, 31, 33–36, 38, 40, 45

L

Lincoln, Abraham, 46

M

Mexican War, 45
missionaries, 12, 21–22, 24–25, 26, 28, 36, 43, 48

N

neophytes, 28–31 33–36, 38, 40–41, 43
New Spain, 6–8, 9, 12, 22, 23, 24, 31, 36, 43
   exploration from, 5–9
   viceroys of, 9, 24
New World, 5–6

P

Palóu, Fray Francisco, 22, 24
Pizarro, Francisco, 6
Portolá, Captain Gaspár de, 9

Q

quadrangle, 30

S

secularization, 12, 43–46
Señán, Fray Jose, 36
Serra, Fray Junípero, 9–10, 14, 21, 22, 23, 24, 26, 36, 48
Spain, 5–6, 9, 21, 23, 43

V

Vizcaíno, Sebastián, 8–9